That Which Burns

A Law Enforcement Guide to Winning the War Within

Brandon Grimm

This book is dedicated to every single member of Law Enforcement. Those that have served, are currently serving or will serve in the future. Law Enforcement is a profession unlike any other in the world and your continued courage and dedication to serve the community is not only admirable, but also appreciated.

Thank you & stay safe!

Thank you to J.G. & K.C.

I want to thank my parents for their unwavering support, love and continued mentorship over the years.

Thank you to my wife, who encourages me to follow my dreams and challenges me to be the best version of myself.

The biggest thank you to my children. I love you each more than you will ever know "BIGBOY", "Mr. O" and "Cookie".

To those we have lost:

"EVERY MAN'S HEART ONE DAY BEATS ITS FINAL BEAT. HIS LUNGS BREATHE THEIR FINAL BREATH. AND IF WHAT THAT MAN DID IN HIS LIFE MAKES THE BLOOD PULSE THROUGH THE BODY OF OTHERS AND MAKES THEM BELIEVE DEEPER IN SOMETHING THAT'S LARGER THAN LIFE, THEN HIS ESSENCE, HIS SPIRIT, WILL BE IMMORTALIZED BY THE STORYTELLERS. BY THE LOYALTY, BY THE MEMORY OF THOSE WHO HONOR HIM AND MAKE THE RUNNING THE MAN DID LIVE FOREVER"

-THE ULTIMATE WARRIOR-

Contents

The Wood & The Flame

"What is going on with you?", a shift mate asked me one day as we were in the locker room changing out after shift. "You haven't been acting like your normal self lately". I just shook my head in agreement. "I don't know. I'm just over it all, I guess", I replied. The thing is, I couldn't give a better answer because I did not even know what was going on with me or why I was different from how I had always been. I was just there....existing. I did not feel as in control of my emotions as I previously had felt.

As I reflect on my days in law enforcement, it makes me wonder...was I the wood or the flame? This is a weird question, but with the context I'll provide throughout this book, each of us will be able to answer it.

There is a default position that we tend to gravitate toward during the many situations and circumstances we experience not only in life but in law enforcement. Which one is better to be though? The wood or the flame? First, I want to be clear about who this book is for and what exactly it is/isn't. I'm writing this book as someone who has spent most of his adult life in the world of law enforcement. It is the life and world I know and lived in until I left in 2019. I'm writing this book from the perspective of and based on the experience of a law enforcement officer. Or Police Officer. Or Cop. Whatever term you want to use.

If you are a current or former member of law enforcement or someone with aspirations to become a member of law enforcement, then this book is for you. If you are the spouse, family member, or friend of someone that fits the description above, then I want to tell you that you are safe here as well. You each should feel right at home as we progress through these pages, which is important because, as you all know, there aren't many places in our society in which we feel right at home…not anymore anyway.

Whatever thoughts and emotions come from reading this book are safe with me because they are likely the same thoughts and emotions I have felt while serving or while writing this book.

Next, I realize not everyone reading this book will fit those criteria. Maybe you are someone that knows me, and you wanted to check this book out because you have read my first book, *As I Walk*. If this is you, then I want to just say thank you for reading this and you are still welcome here. I hope there are still some valuable takeaways for you even if many of the topics I will cover or stories I will share might sound a bit foreign to you.

If you are someone that was given this book by another person that feels you should read it, I want you to let your guard down for a moment and dive in with both feet.

On to the second question. What is this book? This book is not an instruction manual and it should not be viewed as such. I am not a mental health expert or even a mental health professional. Rather, I hope that it is viewed as an encouragement to support ourselves, and each other and to smash the stigma of mental health within law enforcement.

The sad and harsh reality of this job is that next to nobody is going to take the lead on helping you mentally until you do. That was my experience and the experience of several others that I know who either continue to serve or have previously served in law enforcement.

I hope this book provides guidance on what has worked for others while giving you some tangible ready-to-use resources. New tools at your disposal and gear for your mental duty belt. When I experience situations pertaining to my mental health now, I am more equipped than ever before due to using tools found in this book. This allows me to manage myself in a healthy way. Again, until you are ready to be honest with yourself and take control of this area of your life, your mental health will never improve.

We will work through a very clear timeline in this book that each of you will find yourselves on and where we land on that timeline will vary from person to person. This timeline will challenge you in new ways. The topics will feel heavy at times and that is the point. It is time for each of us to see what feels heavy to us and how we can stop carrying around unnecessary emotional and mental weight. This will require you to take an in-depth look at yourself both personally and professionally to see exactly where you are on the timeline. This will help create an expectation for what could be in store for you in the future. It will also help you find your way to the final phase, which is where we all want to be as you will see. I will encourage you. I will motivate you. I will challenge you. But ultimately, the vast majority of this journey will be your responsibility.

When it comes to your mental health, you are responsible for yourself.

Now, you may be accountable to many others like your family or friends or co-workers, or even the members of the communities in which you serve, but none of them are responsible for your mental health like you are. It is time to dig in, do the work and get stronger mentally as a profession. A profession that is made up of amazing people. You deserve it. If nobody has ever told you that before or maybe even reading me say it to you in this book for the first time makes you feel weird, I get it. That was me at one point too, but I assure you…no, I beg you to believe that you deserve to be the best and most mentally healthy version of yourself regardless of the challenges you face daily on the job.

A quick trigger warning…

This will not be my own professional highlight reel. Any stories I share will be shared in relation to the timeline and they may be comical, embarrassing, and/or graphic in nature. I am confident that each of you will relate to them and understand their relevance. Out of respect for the people involved in some of these stories, I will not be going into great detail. This is also not needed because you each have your own experiences and you will likely reflect on those after reading just a few words of my stories. Ultimately, this book is not just about me.

This book is about you.

This book is about the profession.

This book is about change.

A change that is so desperately needed. A change that is taking too long to take shape. A change that will save lives, change lives, and get lives back to where they should be. A change that must break down the walls of tradition and unwritten rules. A change that will begin to grow the profession in a way like never before.

This book is based on an analogy that I am confident will lead to a valuable perspective change for each of us. The analogy is based on two roles or characters that I will bring to life for you. The way these two characters interact with each other over time mirrors the typical career progression in law enforcement when it comes to mental health. Each of them is valuable on their own, but they need each other to reach their full potential.

Allow yourself to have an open mind in terms of role assignment here. Trust me, you play the role of one of these characters anytime you experience a troubling situation on the job. Think about which one you are and which one you should be as we travel through these pages together.

Let's talk about the wood. I want you to think of a pile of chopped wood that is ready to be used for a campfire. This can be the type of wood pile that looks like a mound of wood, where the pieces are just thrown on top of each other making a pyramid of firewood. The wood pile can also be one where the wood is neatly stacked on top of each other in rows, the type that you sometimes see close to the side of the garage, or in my case, I am seeing this wood pile on the back edge of a campsite.

The individual pieces of wood are hard and dense, but together they make an even harder group. Now that we have our wood pile, I want you to visualize one piece of wood. It can either be the sliced in half type that has a frayed interior and bark-type exterior or a round-shaped log-type piece of wood. Give yourself the freedom to visualize exactly what this piece of wood looks like.

Have an open mind here and get the image of this piece of wood stuck in your mind for the remainder of this book. It is vital to visualize this. If you have to, either in the margins here or on a separate piece of paper, write down exactly what this piece of wood looks like. It will be helpful as we continue marching through this. This piece of wood has layers to it. A harder exterior and softer interior. That exterior shield protects the inside from harm's way. Now, it is important to make the piece of wood that you are imagining, to be a somewhat freshly cut piece and not an older, life-less piece. The softer interior still has a decent bit of moisture in it. This is where the life of the wood is found.

Next, we meet the flame. Think of a fire that you have sat by and watched the flames dance all over the fire pit. They sometimes seem chaotic and unpredictable. Relentlessly moving back and forth as they shine a light on the darkness that surrounds them. Ever changing as they move from side to side and up and down often changing directions in an instant. Methodically and forcefully penetrating anything in its path.

Imagine that piece of wood is placed into the fire and being touched by the flames for the first time. The initial burn begins to change that outer shell that it has worked so hard to maintain. The wood is scarred and will never be the same again. The flame breaks it down enough to get further and further inside, while removing all signs of life from the inner parts of the wood until the wood becomes dryer and harder. As the wood continues to sit defenseless in the grips of the flame, it will ultimately get broken down into pieces, or a shell of its former self, while fueling the flames even more. This allows the flame to burn even brighter and hotter.

The wood is often randomly selected for the fire. Sometimes, each piece of wood is looked at to see which one is ready to be put in the fire. In this scenario, we often default to being the wood. As the wood, we are selected for the fire in what appears to be a random act of selection. It is as if we have no control over this at all. Placed into an ever-changing environment without our choosing. Knowing all along that this new environment will begin to change us and alter not only what we appear to be on the outside, but who we are on the inside. How often do we see this exact scenario play out on the job?

Think about it. If you are honest, I am sure that at some point in your life, you have felt like you were randomly placed into a situation that would go on to change who you were as a person. You did not choose to be in that situation, but there you were. Feeling the effects of the stressors and trauma of an ever-changing, chaotic, relentless, and painful situation.

The grief you felt and likely still feel due to the loss of a loved one.

The pain of a broken heart that was the result of a relationship or friendship that has ended.

The confusion and uncertainty that comes with a life-changing medical diagnosis.

Sometimes, what we see with our own eyes causes us this same type of grief, pain, and confusion. You didn't choose to be there, but as a result, of you being placed in that situation, you were changed forever by those circumstances. You were the wood, and the situation was the fire. It took me so long to get this figured out in my own life.

In law enforcement, we are tasked with responding to a variety of scenes, specifically scenes that have nothing to do with us aside from our professional responsibilities. I never once responded to a scene that personally involved me or that I woke up that day and said, I am going to make it a point to respond to this person's house today to see them at their worst.

It was always random, whether the scene was easy to process or extremely painful and difficult to be a part of in any way. At the beginning of my career, I did not feel like any of these scenes were affecting me; but they were. This took time to begin to learn the impact that being physically present for these scenes or deeply involved in these investigations would have on me. Even though I was being exposed to some of the most graphic and utterly crazy situations, much like most of you have experienced on the job, I knew it never had anything to do with my personal life. Until I began to show signs of wrestling with the impact of these situations.

I was the piece of wood, placed into the powerful flames of chaos that would begin to change me. I certainly did not choose to be impacted by them in any way. I always wanted to do what was required of me for my job and honestly, get out of there as fast as possible, all while pretending that what I was seeing or doing was normal. It wasn't. It was required for the job, but it was far from normal for any human being to experience.

This type of change could take place anytime and anywhere. Sometimes, I would even be at home in my bed and asleep when the phone would ring. There I was, a randomly selected piece of wood from the wood pile, only to be placed into the fire. You see where this analogy comes in perfectly now don't you?

Think about your own life. Think about the last time you were simply a piece of wood in the wood pile as you go through your day-to-day routines. Next thing you know, you are in the middle of a fire. It was my experience for quite some time to play the role of the wood and not do anything about it. Stuck in a position that I was placed in due to the circumstances.

Now that we have laid the foundation for the main image that I want you to have in your head while reading the remainder of this book, it is time to discuss the elephant in the room. A topic that is too taboo in almost every department to discuss with the openness needed for real progress.

1

The Elephant in the Room

F or far too long, there has been a giant elephant within law enforcement agencies all over the world. It is rarely acknowledged or talked about, but it is there. Wreaking havoc and changing lives under an endless number of disguises. It is important to not only name the elephant in the room but to also define it and see in practical terms what this looks like in law enforcement. This will help each of us restructure our thoughts on this topic.

So, without further ado…. let's talk about the elephant in the room. Let's talk about…. trauma!

What is trauma? I think we all have an idea of what it is, but I want to start with the actual definition and build from there.

According to the Oxford Languages Dictionary:

Trauma:

1: a deeply distressing or disturbing experience

2: physical injury[1]

Ok, we need to dig into this a little deeper to see if we can make some better sense of this and why this is a topic that needs to be addressed within law enforcement.

According to the American Psychological Association, "Trauma is an emotional response to a terrible event."[2]

So, we have descriptors like "deeply distressing", "disturbing" and "terrible". Whether you are new on the job or have been doing this for years, every law enforcement officer at some point in their career will experience a deeply distressing, disturbing, and/or terrible event. Most of these will be viewed with our eyes but some may be experienced with other senses as well. An ambush while walking through backyards looking for a prowler leading to a physical altercation could easily be seen as deeply distressing. The odor emanating from a death scene is in fact terrible and disturbing. The cries for help coming from inside the building of a hostage situation or the loud sound of a self-inflicted gunshot from a barricaded subject.

Terrible. Disturbing. Deeply Distressing.

It may be one of these events, many of these events over time in a cumulative effect, or all of these situations that cause our bodies to experience trauma. The impacts of trauma can range from subtle to destructive.

This is just scratching the surface of this topic, and we can still go deeper to gain a better understanding of how this impacts us. It is important to note, you do not have to be the person experiencing the traumatic event to be affected. Simply witnessing the event or being present during the aftermath, as is often the case within law enforcement, can lead to similar effects.

What is this "emotional response" that was just mentioned? What does it actually and practically look like?

According to the National Library of Medicine, "Initial reactions to trauma can include exhaustion, confusion, sadness, anxiety, agitation, numbness, dissociation, physical arousal, and blunted affect. Most responses are normal in that they affect most survivors and are socially acceptable, psychologically effective, and self-limited. Indicators of more severe responses include continuous distress without periods of relative calm or rest, severe dissociation symptoms, and intense intrusive recollections that continue despite a return to safety. Delayed responses to trauma can include persistent fatigue, sleep disorders, nightmares, fear of recurrence, anxiety focused on flashbacks, depression, and avoidance of emotions, sensations, or activities that are associated with the trauma, even remotely."[3]

I want to stay here for a minute to talk about flashbacks. Sadly, flashbacks are often misunderstood by most of us, including myself for a while. Flashbacks are not simply recalling a memory in your mind. Flashbacks have a physical element as well. They are more like re-experiencing or reliving the traumatic event, which brings your physical senses into play. Flashbacks are involuntary and are brought on by a trigger which can cause us to feel physical and emotional symptoms similar to those felt during the traumatic event. The triggers can be sights, sounds, or smells (smell of death for example). [4]

These traumatic incidents can produce a variety of reactions that span several domains including emotional (anger, fear, sadness, shame, numbness, lack of emotion, feeling "out of control" or "losing it"), physical (chronic health conditions, somatic complaints; sleep disturbances; gastrointestinal, cardiovascular, neurological, musculoskeletal, respiratory, and dermatological disorders; urological problems; and substance use disorders), cognitive (cognitive error: misinterpreting a current situation as dangerous because it resembles, even remotely, a previous trauma, excessive or inappropriate guilt, intrusive/unwanted thoughts), behavioral (avoidance, self-medicating, compulsive, impulsive and/or self-injurious behavior), and social (relying on or avoiding support systems).[5]

Whew....that is heavy stuff. I will safely assume that you have heard of Post-Traumatic Stress Disorder or PTSD. According to the Diagnostic and Statistical Manual of Mental Disorders, PTSD has specific diagnostic criteria, which is worth the read on your own. Here is a snippet that relates to what we are breaking down in this chapter:

"A. Exposure to actual or threatened death, serious injury, or sexual violence in one (or more) of the following ways:

1. Directly experiencing the traumatic event(s).

2. Witnessing, in person, the event(s) as it occurred to others.

3. Learning that the traumatic event(s) occurred to a close family member or close friend. In cases of actual or threatened death of a family member or friend, the event(s) must have been violent or accidental.

4. Experiencing repeated or extreme exposure to aversive details of the traumatic event(s) (e.g., first responders collecting human remains: police officers repeatedly exposed to details of child abuse). Note: Criterion A4 does not apply to exposure through

electronic media, television, movies, or pictures, unless this exposure is work-related."[6]

This acronym has almost been wrongfully watered down over the years. People include it in storytelling or jokes that mitigate the seriousness and commonality of PTSD.

How prevalent is PTSD in law enforcement? According to the National Alliance of Mental Illness, it is estimated that 35% of all police officers suffer from PTSD. Furthermore, approximately 18-24% of all Dispatchers are currently suffering from PTSD. [7]

To put this in further context, according to the National Law Enforcement Memorial Fund, there are over 800,000 sworn officers in the United States.[8] Even using the roughest of numbers, based on that data alone, we can see that trauma has been doing a number on this great profession over the years.

How do these numbers compare to the non-law enforcement population in the US? According to the United States Department of Veteran Affairs, approximately 6% of the population will suffer from PTSD at some point in their lives.[9] I suppose a case could be made that the 35% of police officers are included in that 6% of the total population and yes, I know the total population and the number of sworn officers differ greatly. The point of bringing up these numbers in this book is to paint a picture of the elephant in the room. PTSD in law enforcement, which stretches from Officers to Dispatchers and everyone in between is more common than most of us probably realize. Not only do the effects show up in the workplace, but they also follow us home to our families.

As we progress through our law enforcement careers, it is easy to see all of these types of traumas and or their related reactions/responses are fair game. All are completely possible or even probable depending on the person and the environment in which we each work.

So, if we go back to the definition of trauma that we covered a moment ago, all of this information pertains to our reactions to those disturbing and distressing events. All of this is related to the first part of the definition, but what about that second part that most of us probably glossed over due to thinking it lacked relevance? What about "physical injury"? Could the emotionally traumatic experiences we go through for many of us in law enforcement cause us a physical injury? Let's look at this a little bit deeper.

What does trauma do to our brains? Great question. I won't pretend to be an expert on the science of any of this and will trust that if you want to know more about it, then you will know where and how to find that information. The scientific advancements in recent years confirm the changes to our brains after an emotional trauma are similar to the changes to our brains after a physical trauma, particularly, in those that develop PTSD. [10]

The three areas of the brain impacted the most include:

- Amygdala- nervous tissue responsible for emotions, survival instincts, and memory (fear response modulator)

- Hippocampus- responsible for storing and retrieving memories

- Prefrontal cortex- responsible for regulating and rationalizing emotions, including fear [11]

When these areas are negatively impacted by emotional trauma, they are unable to function properly. An example would be the prefrontal cortex being unable to rationalize fear that was originally sensed by the amygdala.

Here is why this is important to not only talk about period but also to cover so early in this book.

We, as current, former, and/or retired law enforcement officers NEED to change our thinking on the topic of trauma.

There is still such a macho alpha dog mentality when it comes to the effects of all of the messed up stuff we experience on the job. I have seen several social media posts from now former law enforcement officers in the past few years, where they courageously and vulnerably share that they are leaving law enforcement due to the effects of trauma.

Too many times, I have seen comments from other users that based on clicking on their profiles appear to be currently serving in law enforcement who ridicule and criticize them for leaving. I have seen comments like, "I must be built differently because I have seen every type of messed up scene in my 25 years, but it has not impacted me at all" or "this job is not for the weak" etc. Although I do not believe for one second that anyone that has served in law enforcement for any substantial amount of time has not been impacted "at all" by the job, it is so important to change our thinking from the old school way to calling the effects of trauma what they are…a mental injury.

Not going insane or losing our minds. Not a weakness.

Injury.

PTSD is technically classified as a mental disorder [12], but a quick perspective shift will help us realize that for something to be in disorder, it is possible for it to also be in order. Changing our perspectives from viewing it strictly as a mental illness to viewing it as a mental injury can go a long way in providing hope to us on the road to recovery.

Similar to tearing a rotator cuff or an ACL. These injuries can happen in one single incident or due to prolonged exposure to stressful events, like playing sports or lifting weights.

We must be honest about the science behind this.

The good thing about injuries is they can be treated. Recovery and healing are a real possibility. This is huge for us all. Just like the torn ACL or rotator cuff, I mentioned a second ago, our brains suffer injuries that require healing and treatment. What that treatment looks like, I will dive more into that in a bit, but I hope that this section of the book causes all who read it to stop and think about the idea that it is an injury, rather than a weakness or illness.

Maybe you are sitting here reading this chapter and you are checking every box when it comes to the symptoms I covered. Maybe you are like, "wow, some of those symptoms have shown up in my life" or "I have been struggling with these things". Not only are you not alone, but you are in the right place my friend!

Now, we are going to walk through an all-too-common timeline or progression of our careers in law enforcement. This was not only based on the timeline of my career, but also the careers of several other former members of law enforcement that I have spent time breaking this down with over the years.

For most of us who spent at least a few years on the job, doing anything other than working in law enforcement was only something we thought of when frustrated, but not something we ever seriously considered pursuing. I'd guess almost nobody in law enforcement has spent much time thinking about having their brains injured on the job mentally by what they have to see or do each shift. This lack of thinking about the topic of trauma can likely be traced back to the beginning of each of our careers. It is rooted deeply in a lack of preparation.

2

Unprepared

The chopped wood is stacked in the wood pile. Nothing about the wood's current state would lead it to believe that it will eventually be burnt by the flames.

F rom all that I can tell, I had a relatively normal start to my law enforcement career. After graduating college in December of 2007, there was a period of a few months without a grown-up job or even a plan on what I wanted to do. I spoke with a mentor of mine, whom I had met in one of my classes at college. This mentor also landed me an internship with his police department the summer before. The internship required 150 hours of observation and conversations, which were mostly spent doing ride-alongs with the Patrol Officers.

This was a smaller department with 12-15 full-timers from what I can remember. They weren't running call-to-call and based on the city layout, they spent a good amount of time doing traffic. I wasn't hooked right away like some people are, but I wasn't completely turned off by the idea of doing this for a living either. Indifferent is how I would describe it.

This was a perfect introduction to law enforcement as the guys were great and always took extra time to explain what they were doing and why it was important.

After speaking with this same mentor about my lack of job options, he recommended joining the Police Academy, which was set to begin its next Basic Class shortly. I mulled this advice over and talked with my family about it. Although I was still not sold on being a Police Officer for a career, I also had no other ideas on what I wanted to do for a living. I had no wife or kids at that time, so I figured it might be worth trying for a while. "What's the worst that can happen, right?"

I entered the academy in April of 2008 and much to my surprise, I had a blast even though it consumed most of my time. This was a full-time/daytime academy, so there was not much time for a social life which was new for me. I immediately felt a bond with my fellow cadets and enjoyed every aspect of the training we completed…except running. I hated running. Always have. Always will.

Somehow, beyond my expectations, I also felt the benefits of the structure the academy was providing me. Coming off several years of being a lazy college kid, it seemed the motivation needed to not only complete the academy but then use that experience to compete for a career was just what I needed. I loved the idea of having to compete for a job the way law enforcement is set up. It reminded me of playing sports while growing up, which made me feel right at home. The comradery between myself and several of my academy classmates was also a comforting experience. That same sports background was brought back to light with all the locker room banter we did. Law enforcement felt like a perfect fit up to that point.

As the academy class ended, we celebrated its completion with a graduation ceremony in front of our family and friends. One of the keynote speakers was a retired Sheriff Deputy from a neighboring county. His speech was not what any of us who were graduating had expected. Instead of giving us a charge forward or some great advice as we were soon to be sent off on our separate ways into the world of local law enforcement, he spoke directly to our family and friends the entire time. He provided example after example of what he ended the speech with. The conclusion of his speech was a directive to those listening.

In summation, he stated, when any of them saw any sort of change in us as the years go by in the crazy world of law enforcement, then those changes needed to be called out and corrected immediately. He talked about cynicism and anger. He described what the changes look like when a law enforcement officer loses compassion and empathy. When they become mad and borderline hateful at the general public. He mentioned alcohol use and depression. He talked about physical changes that could lead to injuries, surgeries, or pain meds. He talked about the concerns and being aware of any possible suicidal thoughts or comments.

For a day that was supposed to be a celebration of achievements and a forward-looking excitement for what may lie ahead for each of us, this was certainly a heavy topic to talk so openly about. I, for one, was not sure how to take that. My initial and natural reaction was to just think that he was some crusty old-jaded copper that looks for the worst in situations. Never me. That is what I thought. I would never display any of those things he described. Anger? Nope. Lack of compassion or empathy? No way. Becoming someone that depended on alcohol to handle the everyday stress of the job? Not me, I didn't even like to drink alcohol. Suicidal ideations? No chance.

Although I never talked in detail with any of my classmates about their true thoughts on that speech, I am confident that I was not the only one who thought nothing he mentioned would apply to our lives in the future. I am also confident that I was not the only person left wondering where all of this was coming from.

Not a single one of these topics was covered in the many weeks and months of training.

NOT. A. SINGLE. MENTION.

If these were so common, or at least common enough for this gentleman to speak about during an occasion such as this, then why weren't we trained or prepared for what inevitably would lie ahead for these very topics? Why did we spend so much time on officer safety, but zero on officer health and wellness? Sure, we worked on the physical side of things with the endless PT we were doing, but not even being briefed on what easily appeared to be heavy and important topics will always baffle me. Time on the range learning about all things firearms related... Check. Time spent on the mat learning all things defensive tactics related.... Check. And more running. Time working on traffic stops in the parking lot.... check. We spent several training blocks on how to stand and march in formation and even how to do an about-face.

We spent a ridiculous amount of time working on the standardized field sobriety tests and time behind the wheel to practice our driving skills. The instructors covered sections on domestic violence calls.

And more running. What to do when faced with a traumatic event that injures our brains? Nothing.

It is important to note, that I am not knocking any of the instructors as they were providing as much value as they could based on what the state had mandated out of the training topics. I suppose the greater issue is the topics that were not included.

After working for any amount of time in law enforcement, we all know why none of these topics were addressed, especially when it comes to the state-mandated training requirements. Officer health and wellness is a taboo topic. It always has been. You can close your eyes right now, I am sure, and picture an old timer at your department that fits the description of most of those topics. The famous "back in my day" type of cats that walk around the departments as if someday there will be a statue built in honor of their 30-plus years of service. The one with traditions as old and worn as the leather gear on their duty belt.

I will always respect those in law enforcement that came before us, but I wish they would have been better prepared on the topic of mental health and wellness. They weren't prepared because the academies they attended did not require this as a training topic. The generations before us couldn't pass on what they weren't prepared to pass on. I'm confident they would have passed that knowledge and experience on to the next generations and prepared them for the real fight for officer safety. The one nobody else can see or even knows exists. The battle between our ears. The endless fight of separating order and chaos in the community is what we are all used to, but what about the chaos and order in our minds? This is a battle worth fighting for.

Now before we continue, it is important to break this down for just a minute. Notice, in that graduation speech, the speaker did not say IF any of these changes take place.

He said WHEN those changes occur.

When they are visible to those around us. When they become obvious and in need of discussion. For those of you who are reading this and failed to see this the first time, don't be ashamed because neither did I. Not during the speech and not for several years after until a family member of mine reminded me of that speech and started to point out the changes he saw in me. Changes that should have been predictable, but without any formal training regarding these changes, went unnoticed for quite some time.

That is the scary part. He was referring to the changes that are visible to those on the outside. These changes on the outside do not often appear at the same time as the changes that take place on the inside.

For far too many of us, the beginning of our careers reminds me of a brand-new computer. One that is fresh out of the box, and all set up on your desk ready to follow commands and complete the tasks that are asked of it on a moment's notice. It is all shined up on the outside, likely, in the best shape it has ever been in or ever will be again. This computer is available 24/7 and rarely is given the time to fully turn off before being put back to work. The computer isn't even fortunate enough to rest in sleep mode as much as it should. Every task that this computer is asked to complete, creates a new file that is stored within the computer's memory.

Over time there is an accumulation of files, some larger and more significant than others. Some of these files are very minor historical entries of what this computer has been up to. All of this is normal business for a computer like this. Nothing out of the ordinary as these actions up to this point have been simple commands to follow and simple tasks to complete. There is a problem with this computer though. The problem with this computer is not the lack of features or "bells and whistles". No, it has been prepared in the factory to complete every task and do so efficiently and effectively. The problem is that this computer was not prepared with any tools for defending itself against an internal attack.

This computer was never given the courtesy of being prepared with a firewall. No virus protection. No spam and malware detection abilities. This computer is unable to detect and defend itself against the onslaught of attackers to its operating system. What happens to this computer over time? Due to this lack of preparation, the computer is now susceptible to suffering a major blow from a virus which alters it forever. It is also vulnerable to smaller attacks that will begin to break it down over time.

Now, the computer may function properly for a while, maybe even for a long time. It may show no signs of damage and it may leave you thinking that everything is perfectly fine inside that computer.... until it is attacked internally and can't defend itself.

Everything can appear to be working properly within our bodies, specifically, our brains as we discussed in the previous chapter. The turn for the worse is only one call away. It can hit us at any given moment based on what we see each day. Without the proper preparation on what to do before this internal attack or even worse yet, what'to do after the attack ensues and causes damage, we are left defenseless, vulnerable, and left to find some sort of relief typically in unhealthy ways.

This is the type of computer that I was when I first started and how I functioned over the following 10-plus years. Sadly, for many of you, this computer, with all of its missing defense mechanisms and an inability due to a lack of preparation to detect threats, is all too relatable to your careers as well.

What happens to the computer once it has been damaged? Is it thrown to the side and labeled damaged goods only to eventually be replaced by a newer and similar version of itself?

The sad reality is mental health in law enforcement is a very serious issue that has not been taken seriously over the years. It has not been talked about seriously. It has not been funded seriously. It has not been trained seriously. It has not been viewed by those that could provide valuable resources seriously. It just hasn't and we all know this.

Think back to your own academy experiences. Were you trained on anything related to mental health? How about dealing with trauma? If you were, compare the hours of training on this topic to all the other topics covered. How does it stack up? If you were not trained on mental health-related topics, ask yourself why not? If time was crunched to fit it all in, what could have been shortened or eliminated and replaced with training related to resolving our trauma?

3

Unaware

The wood has been randomly selected from the wood pile and placed into the fire. Due to the lack of preparation, the wood has no idea what is about to occur or how it will be changed by the flames.

My academy classmates and I all went our separate ways after that graduation ceremony as we each sought to begin our journeys inside the blue family. I was hired a month or so later as a Patrol Officer at the same department I had done my internship with. When I began my first Patrol job, I was still not entirely sold on the idea of this being my career let alone my lifestyle going forward, but it did not take long for me to get hooked on the fun parts of the job. I made it through their training program and began working the road in my own cruiser. The love for the job and the greater law enforcement community began to take shape.

I felt naturally comfortable speaking with people on calls and asking questions to get more information, making decisions based on that same information, and relaying those decisions to others. The basics of Call Handling 101. Writing reports also felt comfortable to me, which was a bit surprising, given my lack of interest in writing anything in my life up to that point.

Tactically? Well, in this area of law enforcement, I was green. Hot mess type of green. Some would say greener than goose poop! Like parking in front of a house and slamming my car door shut for a prowler call green. Like how do I go to the bathroom with all of this gear on green. I even remember asking my Field Training Officer how I was supposed to stay ready for calls if I have to take my entire belt off just to use the bathroom. He politely laughed and said, "You'll figure it out". Oh, you need to walk back inside to grab your shoes and coat before I take you to jail? Sure, go ahead. Like getting a shell lodged in the Sergeant's brand-new shotgun because I put it in backward while on the range type of green. Sigh. New guys, right?

Yes, I was that guy for some time. I learned a few things in the academy, but there is nothing like real on-the-job training and experience, especially with anything related to officer safety and tactics. I was also a bit of a mess with talking on the radio, especially in the car. My attention span was tested early on. Taking in the sights and sounds of driving around on patrol often meant not hearing a single word of what was being said on the radio, let alone missing opportunities when I was the one who should have been talking. For example, I was working night shift one night and a car went flying by at over 70 in a 25.

Without calling it in at all, I saw that car and just took off after it lights and sirens. It turned right down a street that was connected to the main road we had been traveling on. The side street was shaped like a "U", so I knew if they kept going, they would come back out to the main road at the next street, so I sat and waited in between the streets…and waited and waited and waited. Still not even touching the in-car mic. The car never came back out to the main road, so I turned around and went down the first side street. The car never made the turn at the bottom of the "U" and was now crashed up against the tree.

Still not even having touched my in-car radio, I parked behind the crashed car and walked up to it (portable probably off still!) and go figure it was empty. Then, in my evergreen new guy-ness, I called in that I'll be out with a single-vehicle crash. No mention of the egregious speeding violation I witnessed. No mention of the brief solo pursuit I just had. No mention of the footprints in the snow running south from the scene of the crash. Just a single-car crash on that side street. One of the other guys working was not far away, so he stopped by to see if I needed anything. A clue. That is what I needed, but did not have at that time.

I'm sure you can imagine his reaction when I filled him in on the details of what happened as he then took control of the scene and began coordinating some sort of organized response to this issue. Realistically, even in a small city such as this, I probably had no actual business being out there running around on my own yet.

I share these types of stories partly out of humility and partly in hopes that you get a good laugh out of them as you think back to your first few months on the job. I am sure, if we are all honest with ourselves, we have each had these heart-aching new guy types of experiences when we were first cutting our teeth. Breaking into the game is not easy. It is part of the growth process from brand new officers to what comes next.

During the 9 months that I worked for this first department, I don't recall hearing or having any conversations about trauma, or the effects of traumatic events experienced on the job. I honestly had no idea it was even a thing back then. There I was, new to the world of law enforcement and completely unaware of any mental struggles that any of the officers I worked with, trained with, or just chatted with in passing.

Some officers seemed happier and more energetic than others. Some seemed ready to be done with the profession and move on to something else, but nobody left during that time. Any complaints or unhappiness about the job seemed like normal venting to me, but I kind of just thought it was part of the job. To say I was naïve at that time would be an understatement. Based on the many conversations I have had with so many of you over the years, it is fair to say most, if not all of us, spent time in this unaware phase at some point in our careers.

4

Unaffected

There is a period, often very brief, but it does exist, where the wood is not affected by the fire as the flames dance around and on the wood for the first time.

"New guy, bring me the CPR mask!", my Field Training Officer said. I looked down at the floor and noticed the elderly woman lying there was clearly already deceased, but still, I went back outside to get the mask. This was in June of 2009, and I had recently been hired at a new department almost 3 times the size of the previous department. This was my break into what felt like a big-time police job. I fell in love with the department and the city almost immediately. The field training process at this department was more rigorous and thorough and I was fully engaged in sponge mode, soaking up every single detail I could from the training officers and all the others I worked with.

Off to grab the portable CPR mask my FTO kept in his duty bag. The entire walk down the stairs, into the foyer, out of the house, and to the patrol car was spent confused as to what on earth we were going to do, rather, what on earth he was going to make me do, with this CPR mask when the woman was already dead. Even though this was my first body and years before becoming a Medicolegal Death Investigator, I could tell she had been dead for several hours by that point. This did not seem like rocket science from what I could see.

I walked back into the house and up the stairs to give him the case that contained the mask. He grabbed it and looked at the woman's husband and asked him if he wanted us to try to do CPR just in case. The husband declined and thanked us both for our efforts and our willingness to do whatever it took to save his now-deceased wife.

After we cleared the scene, I was apprehensive to even ask what that was all about, but I had to know. Maybe there was some sort of training value beyond what my common sense told me was a very stupid thing to do.

"Soooo, what is with the CPR mask thing?", I asked.

"Dog and Pony show, bro", my FTO replied.

"Dog and what?" I had to ask.

"Dog and pony show. Not one of us in that house thought using the CPR mask to try to revive an already deceased person was a good idea. But to make us look good in front of her family members and to make them feel better knowing that their police department was willing to do anything and everything to help them in that moment is what it's all about! It's a dog and pony show!" he explained.

This was one of the early moments of my career where I should have realized that I had no idea what I was getting myself into. "That feels a bit messed up to me, but maybe that is how things are supposed to go!" is all I kept telling myself in my head.

There is such an art form to the ins and outs of being a Police Officer. The vast majority of it goes well beyond the training and classroom work we all completed in the Police Academy. The nuances take years to learn and even more years to master if that is ever even possible because the job is constantly evolving with the changes that take place in this crazy world of ours. You all know this. If you were never directly told this when you first started, I am sure you have heard the old saying that goes something like, "Forget all of the stuff they taught you in the academy. It is useless and you will only learn this job by doing it." There is a lot of truth to that statement, even if it is exaggerated to some extent.

Although this was not my first call as a Rookie Patrol Officer, this was my first death scene. I treated this call like every other call during my field training period. I wanted to get as much training value as possible out of every single call I went on with an FTO because I knew at some point, I would be there handling most of these situations by myself.

My training period consisted of some day shift, some afternoons, and some night shift. Afternoons quickly became my favorite, but I was sent to night shift right after field training. Weekend night shift no less. The shift was full of the top go-getters in the department. To keep up with this group was nearly impossible for someone who was still technically in their first year, let alone fresh out of field training with this department. This group of officers could not have been more helpful though. From the Sergeant down to the lowest guy, well second lowest once I came around, they put me under their wings, and I finally started feeling like I was learning how to be a real cop.

By the simple nature of their influence, I became very active, especially in self-initiated work. After each of them would clear a stop, I would send them an IM asking what they had. I wanted to learn from them and mirror what they were doing. This group was always getting into something on traffic stops. You name it and they were finding it and most of the time off very basic PC. They seemed to have it down to a science. I really wanted to keep up with them, especially in those traffic stops, until I started doing walk-and-talks within the apartment complexes. Never in the role of Patrol Officer did I feel more at home than when I was walking around the apartment complexes talking to people and getting to know the who's who of the community. This was especially true on afternoons and nights. The city's population was just under 30,000 residents plus everyone that came there to shop and work each day. I was obsessed with learning the names and faces of all of the frequent flyers.

I started each shift reading the reports of the previous two shifts and looking up every involvement we ever had with anyone they dealt with that day. I wanted to know everything about everyone that we frequently interacted with regardless of how long ago that interaction took place. Ran from a traffic stop 12 years ago? I wanted to know about it. Hid a rock in your sock 3 years ago. A mental note was made in case I ever see you on a stop.

This also came in handy when talking shop with the boys in the locker room. I would hear names come up and I could ask them questions about some of the reports I had read or be able to hold conversations with them about the comings and goings of our usual clientele. Faces. Nicknames. Addresses. I wanted it all. It became a weird obsession for me at times. If someone got on the radio and asked, "what is the name of the guy from the bar fight last year that pulled out a knife on so and so?" I wanted to be the one with the answer. I never kept any of this information in a notebook or computer file, I simply forced myself to remember it. Being one of the "name guys" was something I enjoyed and an area where I felt I could be the most valuable version of myself.

Over the years I learned, there are two types of cops. The first are the cops that remember every name, face, incident, and story for their entire careers. You just simply mention a name or something even remotely close to the name of someone you have dealt with, and that cop will tell you their entire life story including who they have kids with, where they used to live, and how they chased them back in the day. Then there is another type of cop. The one who doesn't remember anything about anyone or any place after clearing a call. They either don't have the gift of a great memory or simply don't care to have all that information, most of it useless, rolling around inside their heads. I am sure you know which one of these two types of cops you are, and I am not entirely sure which one is better off!

The lifestyle of being a cop had sucked me in, although I tried to play it off as most people do. I started working overtime galore. Stopping into the PD on my off time to chum it up with others or to see what they were up to since I was just "driving by". Randomly turning on my portable at home, which could pick up the radio traffic to see if anyone was up to something fun. All the things. For the first time, I felt like I was a part of something bigger than myself. In reality, I was, and we all know that to be true but this type of comradery and sense of community can be dangerous if not harnessed and channeled in a healthy way.

The calls and crashes were strictly business for me, especially off duty. I don't remember ever dwelling on any of the scenes or calls I was on early in my career (first 1-3 years). I was several dead bodies in at this point and nothing about working a death scene seemed to stick with me, regardless of how bad it smelled. I talked with friends and family about the job a lot, in part because of the non-stop questions they all had in the early years, but also because at that time, I felt that was who I was at my core, who I had become. It was all very exciting to me. I could not wait to find ways to interject stories from my shifts into conversations. It was exciting for them also as I was bringing them behind the scenes of a world they knew little about aside from TV shows. Truth be told, I felt different from everyone else. Better? Maybe. Different? Absolutely.

The first couple years of my career moved along at a normal, but rapid pace I would guess. When we think back to our first couple of years on the job, I am sure it is a weird mix of being very memorable, but also a bit of a blur due to how fast it goes. There is simply so much to learn, and the lifestyle requires such an adjustment period that time feels like it begins to speed up. Finishing that first year and getting off probation turns into year 3 or 5 rather quickly for each of us.

From FTO to probation to Patrol to being assigned to the U.S. Marshals Violent Fugitive Task Force to School Resource Officer to becoming a Field Training Officer myself. All in those first few years and I had to sit and think about each of those assignments for a moment because it feels like it happened so fast that it is hard to remember. Now, there is a chance that your career progression in those first few years will be similar to what I just described. Maybe the titles for the assignments vary or maybe you only had one assignment during that time, but I think there is something to be said for the speed at which these few years fly by having a direct correlation to being in the unaffected phase. Of course, there will always be the possibility for exceptions to this for those of you that were affected by trauma very early in your careers.

I don't recall any incidents that caused me a lot of mental issues during this time. I would say I was relatively unaffected by those on-the-job experiences, but the feeling of being different from everyone that I had known or spent time with outside of law enforcement was just a segway from this first phase of being unaffected to the next phase of our careers.

Undetected.

5

Undetected

The flame has started to attack the wood from the outside while trying to penetrate through the wood's hard outer layer.

"New guy, come here! New guy, come here!", I was yelling as I stood at the entrance of the upstairs bathroom a few moments after entry was made. It was the shift Sgt., my new guy, and I on this call. We had just finished clearing the lower level looking for the male subject that had locked himself inside the residence. He told his wife that he was going to go harm himself. The bathroom was essentially at the top of the steps and just offset to the right by a few feet.

As my eyes reached a point of being level with the
floor of the second story, I could see the white floor
of the bathroom under the closed door as the light
was on. I could also see a puddle of blood on the
floor. A quick round of commands was ignored and
we quickly and quietly organized in the hallway. The
last set of commands was also ignored and entry was
made into the bathroom. There he was sitting on
the toilet with a slit throat. As you would imagine,
blood was pretty much everywhere, including on the
mirror and shower wall where he wrote "Kill Me" in
his blood. The guy was gushing.

The first thing I thought of when seeing him sitting
there like that was "welp, that's a lot of blood, this
dude is probably already dead". I thought this would
be a great training opportunity for the new guy,
who had only been in Field Training for a couple of
weeks at that point. Here is a scene, that can test his
stomach a bit and see if he could handle processing
through all that would come next with a mess like
that. Then the guy started gargling blood from his
mouth and trying to move his head. "New guy come
here" quickly turned into "new guy get your gloves
on" as the training moment was going to switch from

processing a death scene to trying to save this dude's life.

My new guy didn't have any gloves with him, so he was "politely" told to get outside to direct EMS on where to go once they arrived. At the time, we carried tourniquets, quick-clot, and combat gauze in our pants pockets. The Sgt. and I found ourselves knuckles deep in this guy's neck trying to get the bleeding under control prior to EMS arriving, which, somehow went better than we thought it would. We found out a few months later, the male survived when he arrived on-station to file an unrelated report, neck scar and all.

I tell you this story not to toot my own horn about saving a life. I am sure you all have saved lives as well, which is one of the more noble things the job requires, even if it feels very strange when seeing the people, you saved back out and about in your city.

I also don't tell this story to belittle the new guy. He learned a valuable lesson that day and we have joked about the gloves since, just like those new guy experiences I shared earlier in this book. He has turned into a great cop over the years and has done very well for himself and that city.

This story was included because this was a full-circle moment for me. This was my "Get the CPR mask" moment. In what most of the general public would view as one of the most ridiculous and crazy scenes they could imagine, there I was excited about the "training value" that this situation would provide my trainee. If you have ever been a Field Training Officer, you have had these same feelings before on a "don't see that everyday" type of call. How on earth is that normal?

Instead of feeling compassion or empathy for whoever this person was, sitting there in a pool of his blood. Instead of being grossed out by what I was looking at. Instead of freaking out about what to do next. I felt none of that. Just calmly trying to train the rookie on a weird call which then turned into following through on the lifesaving training I had received over the years. The person himself did not mean anything to me in that moment.

Looking back on it now, it amazes me how quickly in my career I had reached this point of robotically going through the day-to-day with zero emotion for what I was seeing, touching, smelling, or hearing.

The zero-emotion part is important to note.

Zero emotions do not necessarily mean zero effects. These are not mutually exclusive and when I am honest with myself about this time in my life, the changes and effects of the job were present in every aspect of my life even if they went undetected at the time.

I was somehow functioning in a constant state of fatigue. My patience on calls was growing thinner and thinner. Cynicism had crept its way into my daily life. I no longer believed anything that anyone said as I have spent every day of the last few years getting lied to by people on the job. I was angry at the outside world for not understanding what police officers go through. I was also angry that the non-cops that I knew, either family or friends or acquaintances were not more supportive of all that police officers do. I lacked overall compassion or empathy for anyone and everyone.

I began to hate any police-related material on social media or TV shows, news channels, and even online articles. All of it. None of them had any idea what the job was like anyway. I hated them all.

This was a time in my life, this year 3-5ish of my career, in which most of the friends that I had before joining law enforcement, started to lose touch before falling out of my life altogether. I am sure some of this was of my own doing, either due to my schedule or that magnetic pull we all experience where we only want to be around those that understand what we are going through each day because they are going through it also. Some of it was on them as well though.

I remember a few friends randomly telling me that I had changed, and I was not as fun to be around anymore because I was quieter and more reserved in public at bars or restaurants, etc. I was also told I lacked empathy especially when current events were being talked about and I would offer a very jaded and harsh opinion, mostly that whatever happened to those stupid people was a direct result of their own stupid choices.

My heart was beginning to harden, and I didn't even know it. At the time, I thought this change was maturation not only on the job but in my personal life as well. I thought I was maturing as an Officer and person and this maturation was making me stronger or tougher in some way.

Looking back on it now, if I am honest with myself, I think it is easy to see what looked and felt like maturation was actually disintegration.

I was changing alright, but it was not the growth I thought it was. More like an internal decaying of my emotions. Changed from my former self into a new version. One that was being broken down into smaller and unrecognizable pieces, just like the piece of wood in the fire.

The job has a way of doing this almost seamlessly. Often, we don't even feel it happening. Even worse yet, we think these changes are positive.

Another change I notice now when I reflect on those days is how I communicated with my peers after mostly every call. It was our natural defense mechanism on the job, in the form of that famous cop humor and it began to play a big role in the day-to-day. Making fun of the members of the community after clearing calls or traffic stops was a regular practice of mine. I don't need to explain it any more than that because you all know exactly what I am talking about.

Irritability was more prevalent than ever before. Everything and everybody were making me mad. Citizens. Co-workers. Department Leadership. City Administration. Everyone. We would share cruisers with other shifts. If someone from the previous shift left something in the car, there I was flipping out on them in the locker room, ranting about them in the road room, and leaving the station angry and ready to pounce on the first violation I saw on the road. If the department leaders changed a procedure or asked us to focus on a certain area or violation that shift, steam would blow out of my ears and I would instantly try to find even the most minuscule flaw in what they said.

This is also the time in my career when I thought I knew everything. Part of the reason for this was, for the first time; I began to have some seniority in the department, and having some new officers below me on the roster gave me a false sense of being better than them. I was probably acting very much in line with those that had come before me during their time in this phase. I knew I had changed from who I was when I started the job just a few years before, but what I did not know was the reason these changes were taking place.

And then it happened....

This is the call where I was the piece of wood, and the flames were beginning to break me down on the inside.

6

Unexpected

Much to the surprise of the wood, the flames have penetrated through the outer layer and have worked their way into the wood's core. The wood is beginning to break down from within.

W ithout going into too much detail for the reason I have already discussed in the introduction of this book…it happened.

I had a call or rather, "the call" that brought on even more changes and new feelings, emotions, and thoughts. None of this was expected as I tried to treat this one call the same way I had treated all the others.

As I have described, before this call, I had become a harder-hearted version of myself. Even those closest to me had noticed it.

But this call was different. I found myself in the depths of sadness like never before. Not just never before professionally, but never before on a personal level as well. I'm talking SAD sad. Like crying all the time. Not sleeping. Feeling like I was fully grieving. I remember asking myself, "Why am I so sad? I didn't even know this person."

To say I thought something was wrong with me would be an understatement. I lost motivation for everything on the job. The conversations, jokes and back and forth banter with co-workers I had enjoyed so much no longer interested me. All I wanted to do was be alone while at work, yet being alone was a scary place.

I began dreading doing anything that was asked of me. Shortcuts and avoiding work were becoming a staple in my work ethic like never before. Outside of work, I no longer wanted to hear about, think about, or talk about the job in any fashion. Full disconnect from anything law enforcement related. For context, at this point, I was assigned to the Detective Bureau and had real aspirations of becoming a Sergeant during the next opportunity for a promotion. Our department's Detectives were not promoted positions, rather they were based on assignment. Detectives had the same pay and the same union as the Patrol Division for those keeping track at home.

All of this felt like it was out of nowhere. Blindsiding me.

But, why? Why wasn't it obvious that something happened to me while handling that call? Well, I didn't know what I didn't know at that time. All I knew was that I was messed up in a big way. Everything in my mind felt tangled and twisted up. This is not a position anyone wants to be in that is for sure.

Looking back, it appears the flames had begun to penetrate the outside and infiltrate the inside of who I was. It was all breaking down.

Why this call and not any of the others? I had handled scenes similar, although not quite as bad, as this one in the past. Well, the answer is simple. My brain suffered an injury that day due to trauma. This call was deeply disturbing as it involved the gruesome death of a child.

It cut me deep, especially as a father.

Disturbing. Distressing. Terrible.

The phrase that I will repeat to you as many times as I can in this book…

You don't choose your trauma.

Not only did I not want to talk to anyone about what I was feeling at that time, but I also did not think anyone would care, understand, or have any real suggestions on how to get rid of these feelings. Even the other co-workers that had worked that call with me. They all seemed to be acting fine. "I just need to suck it up and move on as they all did", I remember thinking to myself.

I also felt shame and embarrassment for how I was feeling even though I was confident that nobody else had noticed the changes. "I'm just tired" was my normal response to anyone that asked me how I was doing in the weeks and months after that call. Knowing deep down that I was lying, and there was more to it than that.

7

Unsupported

The wood is now being weakened by the flames to the point where it is struggling to stay whole. The wood is broken down into pieces and has moved into the hottest parts of the fire.

"How are you?", he would ask every day. This wasn't just the casual "hey, what's up? How are ya?" that you mostly hear from others at the start of each shift. This type of "how are you?" was different. It came every morning from a fellow Detective that I shared an office with down in the basement of our Police Department. We worked next to each other in that office for a few years.

Every single morning, he would walk into the office, sit down at his desk, spin his chair around and ask me how I was doing. He would then sit there and stare at me until I answered because he wanted to know how I was doing. At the beginning of sharing an office with him and being asked this question, I would just give the standard "Oh you know, just living the dream" or "happy to be here" in a sarcastic tone before asking him how he was doing.

It took a few months to realize that he genuinely wanted to know how I was doing. Now, even though I was dying inside under the weight of the job and all that came with it, I still would not fully open up to him about everything I was struggling with. This is ridiculous to even reflect on because if anyone would have understood what I was going through, it would be someone who was sharing those experiences or at least who was also present during the many traumatic scenes that needed processed or evidence that needed to be reviewed for a case. Why was I scared to open up to a co-worker, who likely would have not only understood my struggles but would have offered valuable advice along the way?

Would he judge me? Would I be made fun of? Would others know what we talked about and view me as weak or someone that was losing his mind? These were all concerns of mine, even though I trusted this person with my life on many occasions.

This was just a result of the environment in which we worked daily. This is still likely the environment in which many or all of you continue to work in. How did we get to the point where talking about mental struggles makes us feel like we would be seen as weak or the black sheep of the department?

I believe the answer to that question lies in the lack of available resources for Officers, especially after traumatic events. Without having to go home and research online for a therapist or counseling center that specializes in recovery from traumatic events, wouldn't it be nice if all this information was readily available at your department without any fear of judgment?

What if we reach a point where it is on the bulletin board or the wall in the department? Names.

Locations. Resources. This topic has remained too hush-hush for far too long.

Looking back on it, I wish I would have answered his question openly and honestly when asked how I was doing. I wish I would have just told it like it was. "I am not doing well man. That case from last week has done a number on me." I feel this overwhelming sense of regret because now I know, that this same Detective was having almost the same issues I was having at the time from the same types of traumatic events. I now know that he too privately sought therapy and reaped the amazing benefits of learning the tools and resources to combat this mental enemy. We even ran into each other in the lobby at the therapist's and had a true Spider-Man pointing at Spider-Man meme moment.

Neither of us stuck around in law enforcement long after this as we have each moved on to other jobs. After breaking down the walls of fear, we have had many open and great conversations with each other about these struggles. We have formed a bond over this topic and check on each other frequently. And yes, before one of you ask because I know one of you will, he has permitted me to share this even if he is not named.

This type of connection was not only available to us then, if only we had simply talked about it while working together, but it is available to each of you today, especially those who are still on the job.

How does your department handle the topic of trauma or mental health? Is there any sort of open dialogue? Is it talked about in the same way that an injured back, a sore shoulder, or a bum knee is talked about in the locker room? Do you have easy access to any mental health resources that are available in your area?

If you answered no to any or maybe even all these questions, I want you to sit for a moment and think about why you answered that way. Why is it such a hush-hush topic? Providing information on available resources or offering to help if anyone needs to reach out is great, but is it enough? It feels too passive to me.

What about your command staff? Do they initiate wellness checks on their people? I am not just talking about a group debrief after a crazy call. I am talking about them picking up the phone or meeting you for a quick chat in the gas station parking lot. I am talking about that genuine "how are you doing?" that I mentioned before. The kind where they sit there and wait for you to answer, so they can provide some help when needed.

Does your department have a designated area where announcements or current-event types of notices are hung? Do they invite owners of counseling centers or therapists in to do meet and greets at roll call or shift change? Now, this might sound extreme, but I wonder how different this line of work would be if all departments had a therapist on staff. One that was available for everyone to have regular appointments with. One that was so accessible that you would see each other coming and going from appointments much like seeing each other coming and going from the weight room. What if this was viewed in the same way as going in for a weekly workout? What if we got to the point of being that open about it?

Does your state or whoever offers training courses to you offer anything related to mental health or dealing with the stress of the job or anything trauma related? If so and you have not signed up yet, even if you feel you are honestly in the unaffected phase, what is holding you back from being proactive and signing up?

You are the only one that can answer any of these questions for yourself. The reason for that is simple but so very important.

Nobody will fight for your mental health for you.

Nobody.

Not your State.

Not your department.

Not your supervisors.

Not your co-workers.

Not your friends.

Not your spouse.

Nobody will fight for it for you.

This is super important, so stay dialed in here.

You are responsible for your mental health regardless of what anyone else does for you.

This is your obligation to all of those I just mentioned. They are relying on you to fight for this. They are relying on you to be proactive with your recovery, just like they would if you blew your knee out chasing some joker through a backyard.

But what happens if you don't? Maybe that is what you are asking after reading that. "If I don't, then what?"

8

Uncorrected

The longer the wood stays in the hottest parts of the fire, the quicker it will become coals and ash. Unrecognizable from its former self while being fully used by the flames for their benefit.

I f reading the previous chapter prompted you to think to yourself, "What if I don't take it upon myself to seek out the resources that are available to heal myself and resolve my trauma?", then this chapter is for you. We need to cut right to the chase here and roll up our sleeves and dig in. If you leave your trauma unresolved and all of the effects of that go uncorrected, then you are risking so much. You are risking your marriage or relationships with significant others. You are risking your children's well-being by not being the best parental version of yourself. You are risking your career. Simply put, you are risking your life if you stay in this phase. This is no joke, and I am not trying to use hyperbole here. It doesn't take a lot of research to know how serious this can be for even the most "normal" of cops.

I was in this phase for a couple of years and if I could sum up my existence during that time, I would say that I was breathing to death. Just going through the motions.

Feeling like you are breathing to death is no way to live.

I tried to just make it through each day without feeling like a zombie in my own body. A shell of my former happy and valuable self. I thought I was being courageous for sucking it up and forging ahead through the mess. I thought that is what bravery looked like. Show up each day. Put my uniform on. Strap on my gear and go out and do the job without getting myself or anyone else hurt. That does not lack importance, but ignoring my mental injuries was no way to live.

This is the stage where "health problems" take a bigger toll on people. I know this because I experienced it. I also know this because so many others that I have talked to, that have been in this phase have mentioned, they have all gone to the ER over and over or doctor's appointments galore because they were having "health" issues. Headaches. Chest pain. Stomach pain. Ulcers. Acid Reflux. The list goes on and out of the many former officers I have talked to about this and even some that are still on the job, not one of us had any sort of concrete diagnosis from these issues. Most were told it was just stress related.

Was it just stress or was it unresolved trauma?

When we find ourselves stuck in this phase, every aspect of our overall health is connected and negatively impacted. Our sleep is affected which leads to lower overall energy and increased irritability. This affects the health of our relationships in addition to leaving us feeling less motivated to do things like working out or eating healthy. This is the phase when "feeling" sick or injured becomes the norm. Our immune systems can be weakened, but as many of us can attest to, the increased level of anxiety can make us believe something is wrong with us, even if there isn't. You can see how this becomes a snowball effect or our version of the "slippery slope" we hear so much about in law enforcement.

On one of my many trips to the doctor's office during that time, I once again thought I was having heart issues. I was convinced that this "pain" in my chest was heart-related. They put me through the typical heart-related tests (again) and not only was my heart completely fine, but while listening to the doctor's explanation of why I might be feeling this way, I made a split-second decision to say out loud that I was not in a good place mentally and wanted to talk to someone. The doctor and medical student in the room told me to sit tight and that they would be right back.

A few moments later, in walked an older doctor who sat down next to me. I thought "oh great here comes the group hug and kumbaya". This doctor went into what felt like "mom mode" and could not have been more awesome during this conversation. She made a recommendation for a counseling provider that was local and approved by our insurance. We talked through some of the basic details, and she agreed it was time to begin therapy.

For most of us, myself included at the time, the idea of therapy can make us feel weak or like some sort of failure. I didn't even really know what therapy looked like aside from thinking I would be like Tony Soprano sitting in the middle of Dr. Melfi's office. I had no idea what to expect. Sadly, I didn't even know if anyone I knew had been to therapy before. It was a topic that I don't recall ever talking about before that day.

I was so nervous before my first therapy appointment. I remember sitting there in the lobby and feeling the sweat dripping down my sides. I still felt like a failure and a coward for some reason. I felt like the therapist was going to judge me and then somehow everyone would find out that I was a wimp, and I wouldn't be able to show my face around the department again. Ridiculous to reflect on, but real thoughts at the time.

I envisioned the long couch to lie on while rambling on and on about all of my issues while the therapist quietly took notes from across the room. It wasn't like that at all. There was a period of time spent breaking the ice and finding some comfort in my surroundings, but after that, it was very much a "let's roll up our sleeves and get to work" type of inter-action from there on out. This wasn't just some sort of venting session. Having someone in my corner to work through the pains caused by trauma, without any fear of judgment, while learning the tools needed to recover was a true life-changer for me.

My very first takeaway from therapy is the perfect transition from this phase of uncorrected to the next chapter. This is something that I want you to begin thinking a lot about.

Our past, whatever that looks like for you and your life, is a moment in time that should be reflected upon at a time of our choosing and not dwelled upon constantly. Look at it like this…

The past should be a place of reference, not a place of residence. It will always be there. It will always be available to us to check in, but we should not stay there long.

9

Unperfected

Becoming the flame. Making the switch and using the wood to our advantage to become stronger. Using the past experiences for our benefit.

Here we are. We have reached the point of making a change in our lives. Or maybe it is time for that person in your family or friend list that has law enforcement experience to make a change. This is the real meat and potatoes section of this book. I hope that it challenges you in new ways. Stretches your imagination and pushes you outside of your comfort zone, especially mentally. Maybe this is your first time trying any of these things or maybe you have tried some variations of them in the past. This information will be a combination of tools and resources that you can have at your disposal at a moment's notice and keep you moving forward in a healthy way.

This chapter will be heavy on visualizations and imagery so chew on this information at your own pace.

All the techniques listed below are a combination of preventative measures to keep you in a good place mentally and proactive responses for when things are not going so well. These responses can help you get back into a good head space when needed. This is the moment you must decide if you are going to continue being the wood or if you are going to make a switch and become the flame. None of this should be viewed as a replacement for therapy. Rather, this information should be viewed as examples of the type of work you may experience after starting therapy. I hope that these examples make the idea of therapy more comfortable for you.

You will be required to do the work.

Nobody can do this work for you. Someone can guide you in a healthy direction and encourage you to do the work, but you have to do it.

Better yet, you NEED to do it.

Your loved ones and co-workers are relying on you to do this work. To get to a healthy place and stay there for longer durations. It is challenging work, but it is worth it because you are worth it.

You are worth investing the time and effort into getting mentally stronger. You are worth the fight to recover when you sustain one of those mental injuries we spoke about. Your operating system is worth protecting at all costs.

The goal here is NOT perfection as that is an unreasonably lofty goal. We need to be realistic with each other here. The goal is progress. First and foremost, simply, make it to tomorrow.

Each day, no matter how bad it gets for you, the goal is to make it to tomorrow.

I recently saw someone in law enforcement comment on a social media post that nobody or anything will make him feel human again. This is a feeling far too many of us experience in our careers.

It is an awful feeling and one that in the moment feels like you simply can't shake. We want so badly to make sense of the senseless tragedies we encounter on the job. In some ways, I think this happens because it is our nature to want to prevent them from happening to others, but we can't. That isn't how life works and it certainly is not how the job works. We want to find clarity in the most messed up of situations, but this isn't possible no matter how hard we try.

We also want to make sense of why some situations cause us trouble mentally when others don't. It is in this randomness that we can find ourselves engulfed in confusion. This is probably the same question pro athletes ask themselves when they randomly tear their ACL after landing just like they have done so many other times. Or a pitcher blowing out his elbow after throwing the exact same pitch the exact same way he has done so many times before.

Although these athletes will likely never make sense of this, they know that recovery is possible. They know that with time and the work of health professionals, they will begin the healing process. They know that through physical therapy they can get stronger every day and return at a high capacity.

This is also true for each of us mentally.

Hear me loud and clear on this point. Feeling human is not only possible, but it is also very likely when you become the flame and get to work.

The goal here is to show you that there are so many ways to start playing offense rather than always playing defense mentally. This is also not an exhaustive list of what could work for you. Notice I said, "could". None of these are fail-proof. Not the first time and maybe not any time, but each one is worth trying when you find yourself stuck in that uncorrected phase.

I will tell you with 100% certainty that not even one of these tools will work if you do not try to use them.

They should be viewed just like the tools in your garage or basement. Unless you select the right tool for the job and put it to use for what your needs are, then the job is never going to progress. Simply staring at the home renovation job you plan on completing will do nothing to progress it toward the finish line. You have to make an effort to assess the problem, come up with a plan, go into your tool area and select the correct tool for the job. Most importantly, you then need to put that tool to work.

You all do this every day at work with handling calls or cases. Think about your duty belt for a second. You have strategically placed each item on your belt. Each tool has a specific spot for a specific purpose. Your training allows you to quickly assess the problem, think of which tool you need to help solve that problem, and locate that tool at a moment's notice (often without even looking). This happens so efficiently due to the work you have done. This is the time on task that your trainers have probably repeated to you over and over throughout the years. The tools below will be no different if you put in the work.

Ok, let's get into it....

Picture a large storage facility or warehouse. I imagine it to be as long as it is wide and as tall as it is full. The type of storage warehouse that is filled with nothing but filing cabinets. Row after row after row of filing cabinets as far as the eye can see. Each row is labeled with a different category.

These categories relate directly to your life experiences. One row will be childhood memories and inside this row, are cabinets full of every childhood memory you can find inside your mind. Another row might be your memories from middle school or high school. Or memories of your twenties and so on. Each category contains several subcategories. Your childhood memories row may have subcategories like school memories or sports memories, or friends and neighborhoods. Maybe there is a subcategory for family events or vacations. The good. The bad. The fun. The heartbreaking. It is all there at your disposal.

Now, these memories are always there, whether you are thinking of them or not. Our brains store these memories in ways that I am not smart enough to understand. The choice to mentally return to the images and feelings associated with each of these memories is ours and ours alone. Not only do we have the power to select whichever file we want at any given moment, but we are also in charge of what we do with that file. It is our choice how long we want to review it and when to put it away. This is a tremendous power to possess.

We need to revert our focus back to the flame and the wood. This is important because which one we choose to be at any given moment can have a lot to do with what happens with any one of these files stored in our filing cabinets.

Do you ever find yourself thinking about a memory and wondering, "where on earth did that come from?" or "what made me think of that?" or even worse yet, "Great, now I can't stop thinking about that"? We have all had this experience at some point in our lives. This scenario plays out when our memories or thoughts show up uninvited. When we aren't careful, they can creep in out of seemingly nowhere and have a major impact on our moods and lives. This impact can be profound and either temporary or last for what seems like forever.

You may have heard these thoughts, the thoughts that just show up out of nowhere, referred to as "unwanted thoughts" or "intrusive thoughts". Again, I am no psychiatrist, so I want to be careful here and not try to get too technical because that is an arena that I am not trained to fight in. I do want to stay here for a moment though and flush this out a little bit more with you because this is significant. I struggled with these memories showing up on my mental doorstep uninvited for so long. They would just repeat themselves or linger for what felt like an eternity. I felt like I just couldn't shake them no matter what I tried to distract myself with. That was the problem. I was the wood, and the memories were the flame. They were using me for their mission and my plan to try and distract myself to make them go away was just making them burn brighter and longer.

I'd often try to keep my mind busy at all times. Never a silent moment until I would eventually fall asleep. Constantly stimulating myself with noise of some kind. Music or TV or my phone. It was in the silence that I felt the most vulnerable and that can be exhausting. Like getting water in your ear that you can't shake out. If you have experienced these unwanted thoughts or memories, then I hope you get so much value out of what we are talking about.

So, if struggling with these thoughts and memories is the metaphorical equivalent to being the wood, how

do you become the flame? How do you use these
thoughts to your benefit, even when they can be traumatic? Well, let's go back into our imagined memory
warehouse. Instead of doing nothing except trying
to distract ourselves when these memories show up
out of nowhere without an invitation, putting the
thoughts in control, what if we are the ones who
are in control? Although we can't stop our brains
from initially thinking about these thoughts, we can
control how long we stay there. The next time one of
these memories shows up, I want you to think about
it in its entirety. Don't think about anything else but
that thought or memory. Think about it for as long
as you want. You are in control here.

When you are done reflecting on that moment within the memory, figure out which category it belongs
to and walk it back to its row. Find its imaginary
filing cabinet. Open the drawer, locate the appropriate file folder, and put the thought away. Close the
drawer and leave that row. You are done with it for
now. That memory, for any number of reasons, has
been used by your flame to make you shine brighter.
You will feel empowered by this immediately. Every
single time this happens, the memories and those

experiences that cause those memories, become the wood we use to burn brighter and stronger. My therapist liked to reference a quote from a colleague of hers that goes something like, "you aren't responsible for the birds that fly by and poop on your head, but you are responsible for the birds that build a nest in your hair."

One of the worst things we can do is to sit in those thoughts longer than we want. Right in the thick of the messy stuff, letting those thoughts have their way with our minds. Waiting and waiting until they pass, most of the time without anyone else around us even knowing. This can feel helpless and hopeless. It reminds me of that GIF of the man walking up to the game with his folding camping-style chair and he flings that bad boy open and plops down to sit and watch. That is what we do too often with these thoughts and memories. We pull up a chair, plop down and we watch them repeatedly. Sometimes doing so while feeling at their mercy. It can be agonizing at times. That is where the idea of being in control of the files in your warehouse can work wonders.

Ok so you don't like the filing cabinet imagery, or you feel you aren't ready to go that deep into it yet. What other tools can we pull from our imaginary tool belt to become the flame and not the wood?

Imagine a stop sign. We are going to use this stop sign to stop our thoughts.

You can envision an actual stop sign and focus on that for a minute, seeing each of its sides and red background with white letters saying STOP or say "stop" to yourself either out loud or in your mind. If you choose to say "stop" out loud, who cares if someone hears you?

Who cares if that same person asks what on earth you are talking about? That will give you the perfect opportunity to teach them this exercise because maybe they have experienced some version of the very thoughts you were stopping in that moment.

Disrupt the thought (stop sign) and move on with your day, refocusing your attention elsewhere, so the brain does not circle back and start the thought over again. We aren't simply distracting ourselves here, while hoping the thought goes away on its own. We are dealing with the thought head on first and then moving on in a healthy direction. An easy way to remember this is, "disrupt, not distract."

Neither of these methods nor any other method will be perfectly executed every single time. That is why they should be seen as tools or exercises. You are building something in your mind, and it takes time to progress. Just like working out, there is pain in the progress. It isn't always easy and sometimes it even hurts a bit. It can feel messy and leave you exhausted at times, but there will be progress. You will burn brighter and stronger because of that work as opposed to simply doing nothing about the thoughts and memories while they have their way with you.

Sometimes our thoughts can get us all worked up, especially if we struggle with anxiety at all. I wrote about anxiety in my first book, *As I Walk*, while sharing certain times in my life when anxiety and panic attacks were all too common. Here is what I said at that time:

"Anxiety is an unbelievably relentless self-manufactured mental warlord. It's predicated on fears and doubts and creeps into your mind like water seeping through the cracks of a dam. Once your mind starts noticing the anxiety starting to creep in, your mind starts digging around in the thoughts that are connected to that anxious feeling. This mental digging causes the dam to break and the floodgates to open and the attack is underway. The heart rate increases, the body's temperature seems to rise, breathing is altered, and the mind begins racing like a dragster down the track with no end in sight."

If we stay too long, the feeling of panic can take over.

Some of you may have success with focusing on your breathing or "finding your breath", as some people describe it. You can research the many ways to focus on your breathing, including belly breathing. I think the most basic example of this is filling your belly with air in a big full inhale for 5 seconds, holding it in your belly for 5 seconds, and then slowly exhaling for 5 seconds. Focusing on counting each of those seconds may be helpful. There is a physiological shift that can take place when we can slow our breathing. Often the mind will follow the body.

This applies to a wide range of situations. Waiting at the doctor's office and feeling a bit worked up? Do some belly breathing while you wait. Sitting in the lobby waiting to be called back for a job interview. Do some belly breathing. Find yourself all worked up right after you get in bed or the middle of the night when your mind resists your stop sign? Do some belly breathing until you can slow your body down and then begin to work on your mind.

Another tool to consider is to write it down and put it away. Our brains are naturally creative and will have outrageous thoughts from time to time. This can be increased after a stressful event. Often the thoughts that accompany that stress are wild and atypical of what we normally think about. These wild and atypical thoughts can often be ignored and sometimes they will go away as quickly and easily as they showed up. If you keep having repetitive un-wanted thoughts, writing these down can be helpful. Keep a small notebook near your bedside or in your duty bag or wherever you want. Write down the thought, no matter what it is or how weird you might think it is. Write it down on paper and then put it away. Don't sit and camp out with that thought. Simply open the notebook, write it down, close the notebook, and put the notebook away. See ya. On to the next task for the day. This piece of paper can even be taken to your next therapy appointment to review.

These thoughts will vary from person to person. Whenever they show up in your mind, an initial question you can ask yourself is, "Is there any evidence to support these thoughts?" When I was handling death scenes more often than I ever cared to while in the Detective Bureau, the thought/fear of death was showing up in my daily life and it was limiting me in the experiences I should have been enjoying. By seeing such a wide variety of ways in which people's lives were ending, I became fearful that doing even normal things that I have always done could result in my death or the death of someone in my family. You can only see so many random ways people die before your brain begins to get creative with ways you "could" die. These thoughts paralyzed me mentally for quite a while.

This fear only ended for me, when I started to ask myself, "Do I have any actual evidence to support thinking or feeling this way?" Or sometimes, I would ask, "If I were to tell someone else about this thought or fear, would they say based on the current circumstances, that those thoughts or fears were appropriate?" If the answer was, and it almost always was, no to both of those questions, then it was time to be the flame and get rid of those thoughts or fears.

Finding an accountability partner within your department will be a game-changer for you. This can be your "shift bestie" or even one of the old-timers. Someone that you trust and feel comfortable talking to when you are not feeling right mentally. Ideally, the profession gets to the point where everyone talks with each other about these topics. At this point, seek out 1 or 2 others within your agency and you may have to break the ice and put yourself out there first.

This can be when you are car-to-car or in the locker room. I remember standing by the drinking fountain in the patrol room and just randomly telling a couple of the guys that I was in therapy and that it was starting to help me. They were quiet at first and the conversation did not go much further than that at the time. Several months later, one of them started to chat me up in the locker room about therapy as he was considering starting the journey as well.

Having people outside of law enforcement to confide in is also important, but I understand the difficulty in fully trusting that they will understand. For those that have not seen what you all see daily, it is hard for them to grasp the gravity of those situations. This is why I am a firm believer in helping each other within your agency. There is freedom in being able to pull up to one of your shiftmates in a parking lot to talk about how messed up that last call was or how the call from 2 weeks ago is causing you trouble. Someone needs to take the first step and it might as well be you!

What are you grateful for? What is the first thing you thought of when I asked that question? If you are like me, I think of my family right away. Have you ever written it down? This can be done daily, weekly, monthly, or randomly. It can be as official as a gratitude journal or as casual as chicken scratch on a piece of paper that you look at and then throw away. Think about what you are grateful for and what keeps you going each day. Write it down and see it in front of you. Seeing it on paper and visualizing what/who matters most to us has a way of making it feel real, while greatly improving our moods.

Earlier in the book, we briefly went over flashbacks, and it was important to gain a better understanding of this topic as they can be tricky for us to deal with.

How can we become the flame with these flashbacks? A sensation-based grounding technique could do the trick for us here. If a flashback is triggered or you do not feel a part of your present reality (physically present, but mentally somewhere else), finding something to keep us grounded in the moment is the goal. Often these tools can be deployed quickly and quietly without anyone around us even knowing. It can be as simple as rapidly blinking our eyes, rubbing or sliding our feet back and forth as we feel the ground beneath us, sinking into and feeling the chair we are sitting on, rubbing our hands together for a moment, or even wiggling our toes. Sometimes it can be helpful to even ask yourself, "What is my present reality?".

A way to answer that question may come in the form of the 5-4-3-2-1 grounding method. It can be done almost anywhere you are whenever one of these flashbacks (or panic attacks) is active. Here is how it works: 5- Name five things around you that you can see. 4- Name four things around you that you can feel. 3- Name three things around you that you can hear. 2- Name two things around you that you can smell. 1- Name one thing around you that you can taste. Remember, flashbacks can physically activate our senses, so actively engaging with those senses is a way to switch from being the wood to being the flame.

This list of tools is likely only scratching the surface of what could be possible for you. They are not guaranteed, but being in this unperfected phase means you are aware that work needs to be done and you are doing something about it. If you are in this phase, I want to commend you. It takes courage to look yourself in the mirror and say it is time to put in the effort to recover and begin thriving. For yourself. For your family. For your co-workers. If you are on the fence about starting therapy, I hope that you give it a chance. Therapy may last weeks, months, as was the case for me, or even years. Maybe therapy will be something you continue forever. None of those are wrong and will vary from person to person. The fact is though, none of us will know how long it will last until we start it.

10

The Burn

When I talk to other people about any of the topics we just discussed, the one thing I always hear people mention is my level of vulnerability. They always comment on how vulnerable I am and sometimes they even thank me for being so vulnerable in their eyes. The reality is though, being vulnerable is a necessary component of recovery. It can be scary at times, but it is worth it.

The fear of vulnerability can prevent us from resolving our trauma. That fear can feel like a giant wall standing in our way, while resolution waits for us on the other side. I encourage you to become the flame and burn that wall down.

That vulnerability can lead to resolution which can give way to an openness not yet experienced by many of us. Speaking openly and freely about trauma will be a game-changer for law enforcement. It may be helpful to view being vulnerable as dealing with an open wound while being open is telling someone how you got the scar.

This is a key to changing the culture within law enforcement and ending the stigma of mental health and trauma once and for all.

When we do the work and resolve these traumas, there is no need to feel insecure when speaking about them. They are simply moments in time that we are referring back to. When I sat in that chair during therapy, struggling to even formulate a sentence when asked to recall the details of "the call".... that was me finally burning down that wall. It took that level of vulnerability to begin the work. My therapist referred to that moment as tearing the band-aid off and having to dig out the infection for true healing to begin.

I can speak on these topics in face-to-face conversations or write this book because I'm doing the work and I trust the work. Is it always perfect? No. Absolutely not. Do I have good days and bad days? Yes. Due to the work that has already been put in, and the tools added to my tool belt, I know that I can still maximize each day.

On the good days, I know what tools I need to use to maximize those days, which often results in my most productive days. On the "blah" days where I find myself somewhere in the middle, I know the tools needed to still squeeze something positive and productive out of those days. And on those bad days, which thanks to therapy have become fewer and further between, I know that extra work is needed to add value on those days and that is ok. The key is learning to recognize each day or each moment for what it is and knowing that there is a tool or resource out there at our disposal to dig in and make it to tomorrow.

As you progress through the remainder of your career, you do have some choices to make. The first is to stick around and continue to serve in whatever capacities come your way until retirement. The thought of starting over again or not seeing your pension all the way through to the end doesn't interest you.

Maybe you love being a cop but, could use just a little nudge in the right direction with dealing with work-related trauma. This will be the choice for probably most of you and there is not a single thing wrong with that. My hope in my writing and you reading this book is that a fire has been lit inside of each of you. Go on the offensive with your mental health. Become as motivated and disciplined with your mental well-being as most of you are with your physical well-being.

If you do not spend time working on either of these areas consistently, then I am begging you to start. You will become a better version of yourself in every area of your life both personally and professionally. Notice I listed the personal first because that is who you are and the second one is what you do. Draw a line in the sand and make a distinction between the two. Find ways to separate the personal from the professional and vice versa. Treat this like a matter of life or death. For some of us, that is what it becomes. Life or death.

Spend time every single day focusing on the tools and resources we discussed in this book. Be honest with yourself and where you are in this timeline. I hope that the timeline provided in this book will have painted a picture of where you have been, where you are currently, and what may lie ahead for you and your mental health. Exercise your brain daily in a positive way. Communicate with those in your inner circles both at home and at work honestly and openly about where you are mentally on any given day.

Do not think for a single second that no one else around you will understand. Chances are, especially with those in your department, someone, if not everyone else is going through the same things you are at that moment. You have all likely heard the saying, "Many hands make light work." I had not heard that until one of my FTOs talked to me about that when handling a complex call like a bar fight or a domestic with a ton of moving parts. Do your part. Find your role and pitch in for the betterment of the team. This is true with your mental health. Speak the quiet battles out loud with someone you know, like, and trust. Help each other.

For others, you may decide at any given moment, that it is time to move on from life in law enforcement. Some of you may even feel, like I and many others have before, that you need to get out and start over. If this is you, then let me say to you right now that you can absolutely do that. You can without a doubt walk away from law enforcement, find another occupation to help pay your bills and begin to live a new life. It has been my experience and the experience of many others I have talked to since leaving law enforcement in 2019, that after a short adjustment period of a few months to living life as a regular Joe-Schmo, the lack of stress from the job will make you feel like a brand-new person. I know there will be pension and budgetary concerns that may cause fear to feel overwhelming at times, but if you believe in your heart for whatever reason that it is time to make the change then make it.

I always tell people that talk to me about leaving law enforcement that there is a big world out there and plenty of areas in which they can be impactful. The experiences you have gained during your time in law enforcement will stick with you in whatever career you pursue next. They are valuable in so many ways. If this is you, do not be afraid to put yourself out there. Research how to make a competitive resume and aggressively seek out roles and hiring managers online. This is another area that will require going for it in a major way.

I am not advocating for staying or leaving as it will be a decision you have to make that is based on what is best for you and your family. Either way, the one area of your life that I believe you aren't left with much of a choice to make is facing your mental health and traumas head-on. No longer as people that make up a profession that matters so much to our society can we be defensive in tackling this issue.

Maybe you are reading this and you are a supervisor or part of your agency's administration and you have noticed a drop off in the performance of some of your Officers. Maybe they seem unmotivated or more irritable than usual. Maybe you are receiving complaints about them from members of the community, or they are using a lot of sick time, which is not the norm for them. At first glance, it would seem to be a performance problem. I challenge you to apply what you have learned in this book because this very well could be an unresolved trauma problem. Remind yourself that sometimes you have to check on the person instead of their performance.

It is time for progress. It is time to end the culture of being the wood that is in the middle of the flames of trauma. It is time for change.

It is time for these changes to spread through law enforcement like a wildfire.

It is time to become the flame. To be the ones who change the game for those still playing and for those who will join in the future.

If reading this book has lit a fire inside of you to make these changes, then I encourage you to share that information with others.

It is time to be,

That Which Burns....

Thank you for reading!

Please consider leaving a review and asking your agency to provide copies to your co-workers.

Connect with Brandon on social media:

@authorbrandongrimm

Also by Brandon Grimm:

As I Walk: Unlocking the Life-Saving Power of Perspective

#1 New Release & #1 Bestseller in 2019

1. Oxford Languages Dictionary. "Definition of Trauma." Google. Accessed January 10, 2023. https://www.google.com/search?q=definition+of+trauma.

2. American Psychological Association. "Trauma". Accessed January 10, 2023. https://www.apa.org/topics/trauma.

3. National Library of Medicine. Center for Substance Abuse Treatment (US). Trauma-Informed Care in Behavioral Health Services. Rockville (MD): Substance Abuse and Mental Health Services Administration (US); 2014. (Treatment Improvement Protocol (TIP) Series, No. 57.) Chapter 3, Understanding the Impact of Trauma. Available from: https://www.ncbi.nlm.nih.gov/books/NBK207191/

4. Tracy, N. (2021, December 23). What Is a PTSD Flashback Like?, HealthyPlace. Retrieved on 2023, January 16 from https://www.healthyplace.com/ptsd-and-stress-disorders/ptsd/what-is-a-ptsd-flashback-like

5. National Library of Medicine. Center for Substance Abuse Treatment (US). Trauma-Informed Care in Behavioral Health Services. Rockville (MD): Substance Abuse and Mental Health Services Administration (US); 2014. (Treatment Improvement Protocol (TIP) Series, No. 57.) Chapter 3, Understanding the Impact of Trauma. Available from:

    https://www.ncbi.nlm.nih.gov/books/NBK207191/

6. Diagnostic and Statistical Manual of Mental Disorders (DSM-5; 1) 2013. Posttraumatic Stress Disorder. Diagnostic Criteria. 309.81 (F 43.10). 271.

7. Weaver, Conrad. Documenting the Traumas of First Responders. 2021. National Alliance of Mental Illness. Accessed January 10, 2023. https://www.nami.org/Blogs/NAMI-Frontline -Wellness/2021/Documenting-the-Traumas-of -First-Responders

8. National Law Enforcement Memorial Fund. Law Enforcement Facts. Key Data About the Profession. Accessed January 10, 2023. https://nleomf.org/memorial/facts-figur es/law-enforcement-facts/

9. United States Department of Veteran Affairs. PTSD: National Center for PTSD. How Common is PTSD in Adults? Accessed January 10, 2023. https://www.ptsd.va.gov/understand/co mmon/common_adults.asp

10. Shulman LM. Emotional Traumatic Brain Injury. Cogn Behav Neurol. 2020 Dec;33(4):301-303. doi: 10.1097/WNN.000 0000000000243. PMID: 32947370; PMCID: PMC7774817.

11. Bremner JD. Traumatic stress: effects on the brain. Dialogues Clin Neurosci. 2006;8(4):445-61. doi: 10.31887/DCNS.200 6.8.4/jbremner. PMID: 17290802; PMCID: PMC3181836.

12. Diagnostic and Statistical Manual of Mental Disorders (DSM-5; 1) 2013. Posttraumatic Stress Disorder. Diagnostic Criteria. 309.81 (F 43.10). 271.

Made in the USA
Columbia, SC
22 February 2023

12814938R00067